G000079253

THE HUMOURS
OF NOTHINGNESS

First published in 2020 by
The Dedalus Press
13 Moyclare Road
Baldoyle
Dublin D13 K1C2
Ireland

www.**dedaluspress**.com

ISBN 978-1-910251-64-5 (paperback)
ISBN 978-1-910251-65-2 (hardback)

Dedalus Press titles are available in Ireland
from Argosy Books (argosybooks.ie) and in the UK
from Inpress Books (www.inpressbooks.co.uk)

Printed in Dublin by Digital Print Dynamics

Cover photogrpah/design by Pat Boran

The Dedalus Press receives financial assistance from
The Arts Council / An Chomhairle Ealaíon.

THE HUMOURS
OF NOTHINGNESS

GERRY MURPHY

To Bert,
best wishes
from Cork.

Gerry Murphy

20/MAY/2020

DEDALUS PRESS

ACKNOWLEDGEMENTS

Thanks are due to the editors of *The Well Review*, *The Enchanting Verses* and *Reading The Future* (Arlen House, 2018, ed. Alan Hayes), for including some of these poems in their publications. A number appeared in the Southwords Editions chapbooks, *My Life as a Stalinist* (2018) and *Kissing Maura O'Keeffe* (2019).

Thanks yet again to Patrick Crowley for a close reading of the manuscript, and to Ita Teegan, Jack Healy and Tony Henderson, my first readers.

Contents

⬿

Visage / 9

⬿

Visage

after Yeats

Looking in mirror after mirror
until all vanities fade.
I'm searching for the face I wore
before the world was made.

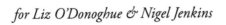

for Liz O'Donoghue & Nigel Jenkins

Pegasus

An age since
a faltering dray-horse
kicked my grandfather's
lights out on Blackpool Bridge
and left him groping
in the Asylum
for meaning and connection.
An age before
I stumbled into verse,
raving blessedly
between truth and delusion
to the sound of Pegasus'
approaching hooves.

Mirror Mirror

I have been struggling
with the crossword
for the past twenty minutes.
Twenty minutes absorbed
in something other than myself.
Still puzzling a difficult anagram,
I begin to pace the hallway.
Passing the large hallstand mirror,
I pause, as usual, to glance in.
For a split-second of exquisite disorientation
(a slow-firing synapse? a trick of the light?)
I cannot place the panicked reflection.

Temporary Abdication

You wake,
to a cloud of unknowing,
a blizzard of lost connections,
all slates truly wiped clean.
You cannot tell where you are,
you cannot tell who you are.
Embalmed in a moment,
without past or future,
name or memory,
need or desire.
Until the panic kicks in
and the accumulation of identity,
the mad pursuit of meaning,
the scramble for signifiers,
promptly return.
The whole shebang
rushing back into place,
fitting you out
with the same stale details,
name, location, time, date,
occupation, social status,
likes, dislikes …
The sprawling entity,
the tiny ungovernable republic:
you.

Three Dreams

IN A DREAM
I am aimlessly watching television,
when three tipsy young women
tumble into the room.
Without preamble,
one of them sits beside me
and presses her face against mine.
At first I am discomfited
and inclined to move away,
but she seems familiar
and totally at home,
and I haven't felt so blessed
in a long, long time.
So, I remain
in the warmth of her presence,
wondering what she might do next.
I wake,
I have been sleeping
with the palm of my hand
cupping the side of my face.

I WOULDN'T MIND,
I don't even have a girlfriend,
not to mind a girlfriend
dragged from a phone-booth
and bundled into a car
by three men
and driven off at high speed.
Kidnapped because
of her famous good looks.

Of course,
with that ineluctable logic of dreams,
I am going to hunt them down
and rescue her
and I'm going to kill
each one of those bastards
who took her,
swiftly and brutally,
Liam Neeson style.

WIDE AWAKE,
bolt upright in bed
and chewing my thumb.
Puzzling out
a heart-shaking vision,
in which a long unattainable
Muse and I,
wrapped at last
in each other's arms –
her stiff white basque
biting into my chest,
my torn-in-two shirt
tangled around her feet –
have just declared ourselves
mutually besotted,
magnificently unsuited.

That First Kiss

That dazzling afternoon,
our first date culminating
in a precarious kiss
across the glinting handlebars
of your interloping bicycle
under the looming tower
of the University.
A kiss that left
a flurry of indignant muses
flouncing from the Pantheon
in its fizzing wake.
A kiss that wiped them clean
from the dusty archives,
as if they had never been.

Aphrodite Radiant

What if you could go back
to any particular time or place.

Listen again in a tumult of anticipation
for the rumble of her car in the cobbled lane.

The familiar whinge as the rusty gate
scrapes on the concrete path.

The dry squeak of her key in the lock,
her brisk steps clipping up the stairs.

The bustle and flap of discarded clothes
as she undresses on the landing.

And there she is, standing before you,
twenty-three-years-old to the very day.

That glossy black hair, that impish grin,
the *postponer of old age* incarnate.

Choice

after Albert Camus

Give me solitude
or the perfect storm of love
nothing less will do.

Apple Nights

for Aileen Barry

I remember
that long hot Summer,
those still, sultry nights,
too humid for sleep.
You would often come naked
into the orchard, in search of coolness.
I would watch, with bated breath,
from the branches of an apple tree,
as you filled bucket after bucket
from the rain water butt
and poured them over yourself,
until every curve and hollow
of your young slim body
glistened in the moonlight.

Café Lorca

I cannot recall all that we spoke of,
except for joking about the scarcity
of white wine in the provinces
after the huge demand in the Paris
that is Aisling.
And the hints, those heavy hints,
concerning the Dark Lady of the sonnets
and your refusal to acknowledge them.
Later, as I slept,
it was as if a comet flared silently
past the window,
changing everything in its path.
I woke, fiercely engaged
with your vivid image,
inordinately cheerful, deeply attracted.

To an Ex-Girlfriend Buying My Book

after the Irish 15th century

Pleasant journey, little book,
to that lovely solemn head.
Though I would that you stayed here
and I travelled in your stead.

Gentle book, it's well for you
hastening to where my beloved rests.
You will see those crimson lips,
you will feel those straining breasts.

And her soft entrancing voice
whose echoes still torment my brain,
will bring you ease, oh lucky book,
while I may never hear it again.

On Her Hair

after the Irish, 15th century

Your dark, intricate curls
would put Absalom's luxuriant
but lethal hair to shame.
In your dusky tresses
a flock of parrots
could nest unnoticed
with a flock of nightingales.
Your perfumed ringlets
invite the bemused poet
to lose himself
and find himself,
then lose himself again.
I could remain entangled
in your black glossy locks
until Time's, or my own,
sorry end.

Broken Date

from a Babylonian tablet, 4th millennium BC

Bilbea,
I was in Babylon
on Saturday night,
hanging with the usual crowd,
in the usual place,
but no sign of you.

I brushed off
the inevitable banter
and joined in the fun,
but I was devastated.
I walked home heart-sick,
I thought we had a date.

So, what's the story?
Is there someone else?
Is there somewhere else?
You could send a note,
you owe me that at least.

Hello?

'Not if you were the last man on Earth,' she hissed
and stormed off down MacCurtain Street.
Later, when I had recovered from the shock
and the humiliation, I began to wonder
who she was and who she thought I was.

A Footnote to the Book of Longing

for Mairín Ní Dhonnchada

Do you remember the cat
in Winthrop Street?
It was calm in my arms,
a warm throbbing bundle steeped
in the late colours of autumn.
Do you remember
the first hint of winter?
The Earth swinging out
to the coldest arc of its orbit,
the early chill rising
to your earlobes –
to your ivory earlobes
your pearl earlobes
your emerald earlobes
your earlobes of snow
your earlobes of brilliant marble
your earlobes of glistening wax
in a sunken cathedral
your earlobes of the belly of the orchid
your earlobes of the bowels of the rose
your earlobes of the tiniest breasts
dangling over the voracious abyss
your earlobes of the ravished nymph
plunged in the primordial swamp
your neon earlobes
streaking across the glass-grey evening
towards the moon
your earlobes of incredible opulent splendour
opening into the high-vaulted caverns of your ears
inside all would be beryl and opal and sapphire

and sardonyx and pure gold
outside the black flag of anarchy
floating on a melancholy breeze.

Random Cataloguing

for James Harpur

On my bookshelves,
between Conrad's *Heart of Darkness*
and Saint Augustine's *City of God,*
a hand-book on Tantric Sex.
I can hear some of my ex-girlfriends
laughing out loud at this.

I can hear all of them.

On the Bedside Locker

after Czeslaw Milosz

A couple of photographs of past lovers
and a handful of poems in their honour.
Without which, I would have been
a philosopher, like everyone else.

From the Paris Archives

for Clíona Ní Riordáin

Spring 1943,
she sits outside
a small sunlit café
just off the Champs-Élysées,
elegant, fragrant, radiant.
Coco Chanel,
waiting patiently
for her Nazi officer
lunch date.

Mozart to his Father

Paris, July 3rd, 1778.
The Symphony was a triumph;
no sooner had the last notes died away,
than I hurried off to the Palais-Royal
where I had a large ice,
said the Rosary, as I'd promised,
and went straight home.

PS: I suppose you heard that Voltaire,
that arch-rogue, has died like a dog,
a fitting reward.

Conversation in a Jerusalem Tavern

So, Jesus,
you on for this weekend?
We're going up to Galilee
for some sailing and fishing
and some serious drinking.

Nah,
have to stay in Jerusalem.
I have a three-day thing on,
suffering, dying and resurrecting.

I'm free the following weekend though.

School's Out

for Mick & Ted Noonan

Three days after the Senior Infants
got their Summer holidays,
the Junior Infants were let loose.
It had been raining heavily
all that morning and the streets
were slick and dotted with puddles.
We, the Noonan twins and me,
must have hit every single one,
smack-dab in the middle,
leaping and splashing and squealing
in a wild exhilarating dance,
all the way home to our aghast mothers
who could scarcely recognise
our mud-spattered faces,
our beaming grins.

Running Away from Home

I have been playing all afternoon
with my brother and sister,
during which I have managed
to upset one of our neighbours
by running through his rose garden.
He threatens to inform my mother;
no need, my brother and sister
are already running home to tell her.
When I get to the front gate,
I can see they have told her everything.
'Wait till I get you inside,'
she calls from the front door;
from the top of the steps
I make my announcement:
'I'm running away from home
and I'm never coming back!'
'Off you go,' she replies.
'Don't forget to write,'
she calls after me
as I take to my heels.
About fifty yards from the house,
on the hill leading down
to the main road,
the presbytery looms
in the gathering darkness,
its stand of cypress trees
soughing and creaking
in a freshening breeze.
Daunted, I turn tail
and run back home.
When I knock at the front door
my mother answers.

'You didn't get far and you never wrote,'
she says, my promised beating
forgotten in her helpless laughter.

New Shoes

'Stop kicking the stones,
you'll scuff your new shoes!'
We are on our way home from Mass
and I am trying to score the winning goal
in the always-running World Cup Final
in my head with every lose stone on the hill
leading up from the chapel,
my last shot
screaming into the top-left corner
of the English net,
almost clipping the wing-mirror
of the long black limousine,
gliding past in a solemn hush,
upon which my father loses it:
'Now look what you nearly did,
are you trying to get us into trouble
with the Church?
Have you any idea who that is?'
From his plush leather seat,
the Bishop smiles and waves,
waves and smiles.

Oh, Ronnie Delaney

for Jack & Kathleen Rodgers

'Will you go down to the shop
and get *The Echo,* a half-pound of sausages
and a pint of milk,'
my father asks.
'But it's not my turn, I went yesterday,'
I wail.
'Ah go on, we'll time you,'
my mother promises.
I take off like a greyhound,
streaking down the hill,
hurtling past Father Lynch,
who shouts: 'On the clock?'
'Yes,' I gasp in reply
and surge into top gear.
I tumble into Rodgers' shop,
get the messages on 'the book'
and start back up the hill.
Back in the house,
out of breath,
in a lather of sweat,
I manage to wheeze at my mother:
'Time?'
'Time?' she replies.

Annual Anabasis

for Mick Buckley

In the Woodford Bourne van,
Danny driving, my father up front.
My mother, brother, sister and me
packed in the back
and swaying giddily from side
to side with the holiday gear.
On our way to Graball Bay
for two weeks in my Aunt's
moth-haunted, ramshackle bungalow.
Excitement building since Douglas,
bubbling over at Carrigaline,
and, as we rounded the bend at Drake's Pool,
holding on to each other for dear life,
we knew we would shortly
get our first teasing glimpse
of the yacht-bedecked sea at Crosshaven.
Upon which we would cry out in unison,
like the Ten Thousand on Mount Theches:
'Thalatta!' 'Thalatta!' 'Thalatta!'

The Apotheosis of Bertie Moriarty

Our geography teacher's third lame joke
this dreary Monday morning,
we laugh loudly.
He chances a fourth, more extinct than lame;
we are convulsed with mirth.
As the general merriment dies down,
an ironic Ha Ha Ha sounds
from the seat behind me.
Into the stunned silence
our teacher speaks:
'So, Mr. Moriarty, you are not amused?'
'No, Sir,' he replies.
Retribution is swift and brutal,
as we have come to expect,
but, in that moment of utter defiance,
Bertie rises beyond mere boyish adulation
into the realm of immortality.

War & Peace

after Yehuda Amichai

It's exhausting:
beating swords into ploughshares,
ploughshares into musical instruments,
musical instruments into ploughshares,
ploughshares into swords.

In the Balance

for Chloe McCormack

There was an interlude,
between the Rebels taking possession
of the GPO at 12.20 pm
and the unrelated arrival of British troops
nearly two hours later,
when the situation could have been diffused
and everything might have turned out differently.
Imagine a no-nonsense Sergeant Major,
already in the GPO buying stamps,
trying to talk sense to the Rebels.
'All right, lads, you've had your fun,
let's just go home and forget
this ever happened, we don't want this
to end in tears, now do we?'
Or, imagine Pearse proclaiming:
'Connolly, what if we've made
a terrible mistake, let's get out of here
before somebody notices.'
But then at 2.15 pm a mixed troop
of 9th and 12th Lancers, on their way
to Dublin Castle to investigate a disturbance,
comes cantering down Sackville Street
and straight into a hail of deadly fire
from the roof of the GPO
and the rest is history.

Job Wilks

after Michael Coady

Were you really the innocent abroad
as Coady imagines you?
The affable clown-prince of the garrison,
flirting with Carrick girls,
getting drunk on payday,
pining for Wessex?
Oblivious to the fraught local politics,
a year after that Fenian bother?
Or just another occupying cunt
the river caught and swallowed?

Fuck You, Milton

for Christopher Ricks

'Nor is England ruled
by the *Scum of the House of Commons.*
It is the Irish who have a Parliament
consisting largely of dregs,
carrying on in the Irish dialect
and repealing the very laws
we passed to lift them out
of ignorance and savagery
in the first place.'

Unknown Soldier

after Paul Eluard

We found him upright
his white brow like a lost flag
of a lost nation.

Shostakovitch

after Peter Bakowski

The nail bends,
not in submission
but rebellion.

Where Am I?

after Boris Pasternak

Wrapped in a muffler, I peer through the pane
and recognise that old heart-warming din.
'Hey! Komsomol kids, playing in the rain,
what century is this we're living in?'

Never be Rude to a Cossack

after Isaac Babel

When Prishchepa defected to the Reds,
his parents were taken hostage by the Whites
and subsequently shot.
Their farm was then thoroughly looted
by their erstwhile friends and neighbours.
When Prishchepa returned
with the victorious Reds,
he set about tracking down
his parents' belongings.
Going from one house to another,
he recovered them item by item,
trailing bloody boot-prints in his wake.
In those houses where he found looted objects,
he left women nailed to walls,
children with their throats cut,
men decapitated, dogs hung, cattle disembowelled
and icons smeared with excrement.
When he had finally gathered
all that had been looted in a huge pile
in his family home, he set fire to it,
cut a lock from his hair,
tossed it into the flames,
and rode off, never to return.

Just Saying

Of Henry Morton Stanley's
many expeditions to Africa,
one in particular stands out.
He was commissioned by King Leopold
to check out the scene in the Congo,
search for ivory and rubber
and determine whether the local population
was ready for the benefits of slavery.
Amongst his entourage
was the whisky-heir Jameson,
an enthusiastic amateur artist,
who, it is said,
bought an eleven-year-old girl
for six handkerchiefs,
handed her over to some cannibals
and sketched
while they butchered her.

Cannibal

for Sean

The first time
I tasted human flesh
I was ten-years-old.
It happened during an argument
with my twelve-year-old brother,
in which he dismissed
my beloved Beatles
as overblown, overplayed
and strictly for cretins.
I lost the plot,
fastened onto him
and took a sizeable chunk
of flesh from his shoulder,
a piece of which
(probably gristle)
got stuck in my teeth.
Howling and gnashing ensued
until my mother intervened.
She was so shocked
at what I had done
she clean forgot to beat me
and sent me straight to bed
without my supper.
But hey, I had already eaten.

Mammon

after Robert Creeley

The Church is a business
and the clergy are the businessmen.
When they ring the bells,
the poor come piling in pell-mell,
cheerful, noisy and stinking.
When a poor man dies,
they shove a wooden cross in his hands
and rush through the ceremony.
But when a rich man dies,
they use a golden cross,
pull out all the stops with a High Mass,
drench him in holy water,
baste him with chrism
and burn frankincense over him,
all the way to the cemetery.

And the poor love it.

A Couplet for Karl Marx

If the opium of the people leaves you in the lurch,
don't light a candle, burn a church.

Tales of Granada

for Pilar Villar Argaiz

In the Cathedral of Granada,
the cardinal's hat hung
high above the main altar
for many years after his death.
Tradition decreed that when the hat fell,
it was a sign that the cardinal's soul
was being welcomed
into the company of the blessed.
On an Easter Sunday,
during High Mass it happened:
the Cathedral was packed
with a devoted throng,
when, during the elevation of the Host,
the string securing the cardinal's hat finally snapped
and the hat began to float downwards
drawing gasps of astonishment
from the congregation.
Halfway through its majestic descent,
it burst into flames.

The Cathedral emptied before it hit the ground.

A Bishop Remembers His Heyday

Ah, those days of my pomp,
early Mass with all the trimmings
in my lavishly renovated cathedral,
mornings consulting with venal politicians,
needy priests and flocks of lowly petitioners,
all eager to drop to their knees and kiss my ring.
Afternoons in the convent,
taking sherry with the Reverend Mother,
gently admonishing an erring novice
on her innocent heresy,
and afterwards the lovely smell
of freshly laundered linen in my nose
as I comforted the magdalens.

Return of the Fraticelli

Imagine the Khmer Rouge in Rome:
salvoes of rockets
screaming into the Vatican;
tanks firing point-blank
into the basilicas;
cardinals in flames
waving from every window;
thick black smoke billowing
from the Pope's apartments;
the Pope himself
dangling by the heels
from a lamp-post in a corner
of St. Peter's Square,
blood still trickling
from his expertly slit throat.

Rain

after Marin Sorescu

It's going to rain,
God mutters to himself,
as he contemplates
a clear blue sky.
I can feel it in my joints,
my rheumatism is killing me.
Yes, there's a deluge due,
thirty-nine days
and thirty-nine nights,
if I'm not mistaken.

Ah, there's Noah,
stretched out in the sun.
Now, what was it
I wanted to tell him?

Let Them Blame the Danes

after the Irish 11th Century

Conor, our King,
surveys his wagons,
heaped with booty
from Clonmacnoise,
as God surveys
the autumn leaf-hoard,
accumulating
in the woods.

The Thirties

after George Orwell

Ah, what a decade:
a scenic railway ending
in a gas chamber.

Epitaph for Francois Villon

The finest poet
ever to have killed a priest
in a knife-fight.

Homage to Paul Durcan

When the history
of the Poetry Wars
finally comes to be written
(the last poet hanging
from the same branch
on the Tree of Liberty
with the last critic)
you will be remembered
as that crazy bandit chieftain,
who rode his horse
up nine flights of stairs,
into an all-night session
of the Literary Senate
and shot out the lights.

Hymn to Stalin

Our Father,
who art in Magnitogorsk,
hollowed be thy name.
Thy kingdom come,
thy will be done in Nizhny
as it is in Novgorod.
Give us this day
our 0.7 of an ounce of bread
and forgive us our dissidence,
as we forgive those
who dissent against us.
And lead us not into Revisionism,
but deliver us from Imperialism,
Zionism, Neo-Fascism and Euro-Communism.
For thine is the Kingdom,
the Power and the Glory,
until the 20th All-Party Congress,
amen.

My Life as a Stalinist

'Capitalist Lackey!'
I shout at my father across the dinner table,
during a discussion on the feasibility
of the Second Five-Year Plan,
the return of Fianna Fáil to government
or my dismal school report,
probably all three.
The conversation stutters to a halt
and for a moment there is silence.
My father's response is laughter,
knowing full well that I am only half-aware
of the meaning of my misdirected insult.
'You're a great one for the slogans, Gerry boy,
try to read a little more
of the literature underpinning them.
In fact, go back to your beloved Stalin
and study his voluminous essays
on this very subject and his methods of dealing
with "back-sliders", "saboteurs" and "lackeys",
then get back to me
and call me whatever you like.'

Between Ourselves

In August 1940,
Stalin sent Mercader
to Mexico City
to open
tentative negotiations
with Trotsky –

to break the ice,
so to speak.

Liberty Quarter

after Jacques Prévert

I threw my cap in the cage
and went out with the bird
on my head.
'So, one no longer salutes,'
said the Captain.
'No, one no longer salutes,'
replied the bird.
'Pardon me, I thought one saluted,'
said the Captain.
'No problem, everyone makes mistakes,'
replied the bird.

The Clock

after Vítězslav Nezval

Time runs away with itself
on Princes Street,
like a mad cyclist
who thinks he can stay
just out of reach of Death
if he goes like the clappers.
You are like
that crazy old clock
in Winthrop Street,
whose hands wind
ever backwards.
If Death took you now,
he would find
a six-year-old boy
in his arms.

for John Spillane

65

Book Burners Inc.

for Mary Leland

Who remembers Sespastius?
He plunged into the inferno
that was the Library of Alexandria
and emerged singed and choking
with a dozen or so manuscripts,
only to be seized by the Christians,
who set it ablaze in the first place
and tossed back into the flames.

Miss Molotov

Because she had walked
through a fuel spill
without noticing,
she arrived at the Peace
& Reconciliation meeting
smelling like a petrol bomb.

In Greece

for John Tripoulas

Another blue sky,
hauled in over Athens
by two men
from the Ministry of Tourism,
is slotted into place
above the Acropolis.
Plato is on the mezzanine
with pittas and coffee,
eager to discuss
last night's disastrous result
for Panathanikos
in the Champion's League;
Socrates, still sulking in his cave
on Philopappou Hill,
because of his depiction
by Aristophanes in *The Clouds*,
rather than the death sentence
handed down by the Council;
Diogenes bewildered
in Syntagma Square,
lost in a throng of honest men,
his fabled lamp finally blown out.

Seville

It's not just the Giralda Tower
at the opposite end
of the Plaza de los Reyes,
its warn yellow stone soaring
into the clear blue sky,
with its piggy-backing Christian
bells clamped giddily on top.
It's not just the unseasonable warmth,
still holding in mid-November,
or those tourists swarming in and
out of the Cathedral.
Not just the traffic hurrying past
the blood-drenched Archivos de los Indies,
to cross the shriving Guadalquivir.
Not the smoky ghost of Carmen
haunting the Tobacco Factory,
nor tormented Don Jose
haunting the Plaza de Toros.
It's sitting at a café table
with nothing more urgent to do
than sip a cappuccino,
dismantle a croissant
and bask in the unstinting light.

The South

after Jorge Luis Borges

To watch,
from one of your
shaded patios,
the ancient stars,
those distant lights
whose names I haven't
troubled to learn,
nor for that matter,
their constellations.
To listen
for the liquid music
as the cistern refills
slowly but surely,
interpret a slight noise
as a bird shifting its weight
on a drooping branch
two orchards away.
To feel the cool breeze
raising the hairs
on the back of my neck,
as it flows through
the sandstone arch
on its way south
to oblivion.

Glimpse

for Maurice Power

Counting the takings
in the inner office,
when the light reflecting
from the coins
dazzles me briefly
and I become convinced
that I have been
momentarily transported
to a former incarnation
as a minor official
of the Tax Gatherer Royal
to the court of King Gilgamesh,
who is simultaneously convinced
that he is living
in a future beyond
his wildest imagining,
with strip lighting,
Page Three Girls
and digital calculators.

A Cranky Buddha on Glanmire Bridge

for Derrick Gerety

Not jogging,
walking briskly into my dotage,
I cross the old stone bridge at Glanmire
against light afternoon traffic.
Passing a family saloon,
windows open to let in some cool air,
I notice a child kneeling on the back seat,
her head half-out of the window,
her hard, unforgiving features
frowning at me,
with the knowing look of someone
who's been here again and again and again.

A Brahms High

for Evelyn Grant & Gerry Kelly

In the foreman's car,
Con driving, Dave co-piloting
with grunts and groans.
Three big men (Tom, Mossie and me)
squeezed into the back seat,
still in our cement-spattered clothes.
On our way home from some
benighted site after a long hard day.
Squeezed so tight we have to move
and breathe as one solid entity.
We are beginning to get high
from the lack of oxygen
when Brahms swells forth
from the car radio,
his *Academic Festival Overture*.
Instead of changing channels,
Con turns it up to full volume
and I am away,
out of the car, out of my body,
soaring into the late afternoon air
above Parliament Bridge,
to the rousing strains of *Gaudeamus Igitur*.

Bands Passing

i.m. Paddy Sheehan

Marching down Brown Street,
hugging the right-hand side
of the scraggly planted median,
proceeding to the sound
of a single drummer,
St Mary's Brass & Reed Band,
trooping proudly back to headquarters
after leading the Eucharistic Procession.
Coming up Brown Street,
claiming the left-hand side
of the median,
the Youghal Pipe Band,
somewhat disgruntled
after bringing up the rear
at the Eucharistic Procession.
Looking dead-ahead,
they pass in full panoply,
neither band acknowledging the other
by sign, sound or gesture.

UFO

What seems to be
a sweet wrapper,
caught in a sudden gust,
whips past my face,
rides an updraught
across Patrick Street
and snags
on the lightning conductor
of SS Peter & Paul's.
Then again
it just might be
a miniaturized star-ship
on a surveillance mission,
routinely skipping
between dimensions,
which has already sent back
an image of my startled face
for processing on Alpha Centauri.

The Little Bang

after R.S. Thomas

In the beginning,
the Floor of Creation
littered with cigarette ends
and empty beer cans.
A few dusty,
kite-like objects
heaped in a corner,
the Golden Gate Bridge,
a thirty-seven-cent coin,
the Marie Celeste, the Marie Celeste.
Some back issues of *Playboy*,
a little crumpled around the edges,
one opened at Miss October 1985.
Forty-seven religions,
six hundred and sixty-six sects,
thirty thousand cults,
one atheist, one agnostic
and one suicide bomber.
Everything ready
to be squeezed down
into a singularity
and set off
like a firecracker.

Globe

after Michael Ray

So far he has stripped
all the outer planets.
Peeling some
like so many oranges
and tossing their peels
nonchalantly into deep space.
Crushing others
and sending the rubble
hurtling through the cosmos,
Blowing the gas giants apart,
to accumulate once more,
streaming multi-coloured winds,
at the outer edge of the universe.

All except one
and now it swings, willy-nilly, into view:
Earth.

Lullaby for Samuel Beckett

for John Minihan

Your mother is singing a melancholy stave
as she rocks your cradle over an open grave.

Beckett Risen

after Dean Browne

The glass re-misted
upright in your yellow bones
hello redeemer.

Rebirth

after Christy Milner

Too drunk to speak,
I left the pub
and took a walk along the beach
to clear my head.
Later, returning to the caravan park
by the cliff path,
I took a shortcut through the graveyard.
Still a little unsteady,
I tripped over a grave digger's shovel
and fell headlong
into a freshly opened grave,
knocking myself unconscious
in the process.
The next morning,
after a deep, cradle-sweet sleep,
I woke to birdsong,
a narrow rectangle of clear blue sky
and trickles of clay
playing over my face.

Voodoo

for Matthew Sweeney

There's moonlight in this,
two lotto numbers
carved into the forehead
of a deaf mute,
buried upside down
in a peat bog;
the polished bones
of seven larks,
thrown again and again
onto the black silk drawers
of a dead Archbishop;
a child's broken rattle
clutched in the severed hand
of an unpublished poet
and *Machushla*
sung backwards
by John McCormack.

Catch

after Eoin McNamee

On the horizon
the super trawlers are shooting
their nets to unimaginable depths,
hauling in unicorns, griffins,
chimeras, salamanders, merfolk,
centaurs, kelpies, manticores,
hippogriffs, trolls, satyrs, basilisks,
gorgons, minotaurs, werewolves,
submariners, shopping trolleys,
the black marble footpaths
of Atlantis …

Myth

for Thomas McCarthy

I'm on my way to work,
the graveyard shift,
four-thirty in the morning,
opening the pool for the un-dead.
Halfway through my panting trudge
up Gardiner's Hill,
I come upon the Minotaur.
He's checking himself
in the wing-mirror
of a silver Audi 350
and snorting with satisfaction.
'But Theseus…?' I venture.
'Never happened,' he replies.
'We came to an arrangement,
he showed me a way out
of the labyrinth,
then boasted to all and sundry,
that, after a brief tussle,
he had stabbed me through the throat,
upon which I had disappeared
in a pall of black smoke.
Suited me down to the ground,
hated that place with a passion.
So, I've been roaming the world ever since,
making the occasional appearance, like now,
to keep the myth alive, so to speak.'

'And you?' he asks.

Dog Star

after Liam O'Callaghan

Sirius glitters
in the empyrean dark
bite me but don't bark.

Conversation Overheard Under a Full Moon

for Louise

'I'm just going to give up,'
declared the brunette
and strode off down Military Hill.
'Don't,' the blonde called after her,
'all it takes is howling.'

And she howled like a wolf.

Intimations

for Brian Crotty

High above the skylight,
moving slowly
across the blue expanse,
briefly intact,
almost anatomically correct,
a cloud skeleton.
Displaying its grim message,
as if for me and me alone.
Then stretching
into meaningless wisps
in the freshening breeze
and disintegrating.

That man,
passing me just now
on Daunt's Square,
looks as if he has
been freshly unearthed
from the abandoned cemetery
in Paul Street.
Bluish to black skin
stretched unevenly across
his protruding bones.
A dusting of clay
still clinging to his
tattered grave clothes.
A blank stare
piercing through me
from his dead white eyes.

Crossing Patrick Street
in October sunshine,
I catch a glimpse
of my reflection
in a disused phone booth.
For a moment
of giddy uncertainty,
I cannot recognise myself.
I seem to have entered
the realm of shadows,
revenants and phantoms,
with the sole certainty
that Death will appear
at any moment
and beckon to me
to accompany him
down Princes Street
into eternity.

Dance

after Nazim Hikmet

I stepped out of my thoughts of death,
performed a dainty little pirouette
and stepped back in again.

The Humours of Nothingness

Not so much a brush with Death
as a playful blow on the forehead
with the flat of his scythe.
Not so much the sound of one hand
as the muffled roar of enlightenment.
Not so much the absence of light,
or the absence of darkness,
as the absence of absence.
Not so much another life
as a four-fold displacement
into something new and strange:
yourself, again.